BOLD KIDS

Parakeets

A CHILDREN'S BOOK INTERESTING AND INFORMATIVE FACTS

No part of this book may be reproduced or used in any way or form or by any means whether electronic or mechanical, this means that you cannot record or photocopy any material ideas or tips that are provided in this book.
Copyright 2022

All images in this book have been reproduced with the knowledge and prior consent of the artists concerned, and no responsibility is accepted by producer, publisher, or printer for any infringement of copyright or otherwise, arising from the contents of this publication.

If you have a young child, you might be interested in learning some facts about parakeets. This small bird is one of the most interesting pets you can get. They are very smart and can be trained to learn all sorts of words.

You might even enjoy conversing with your pet. They're very easy to train and are able to learn tricks and cues quite quickly. Female parakeets can be difficult to distinguish from males. They have a blue cere while their female counterparts have a brown cere.

The most interesting fact about parakeets is that they are extremely intelligent. They remember their names and are able to communicate with others through their body language. You can learn more about this fascinating animal by reading the following facts about parakeets for kids.

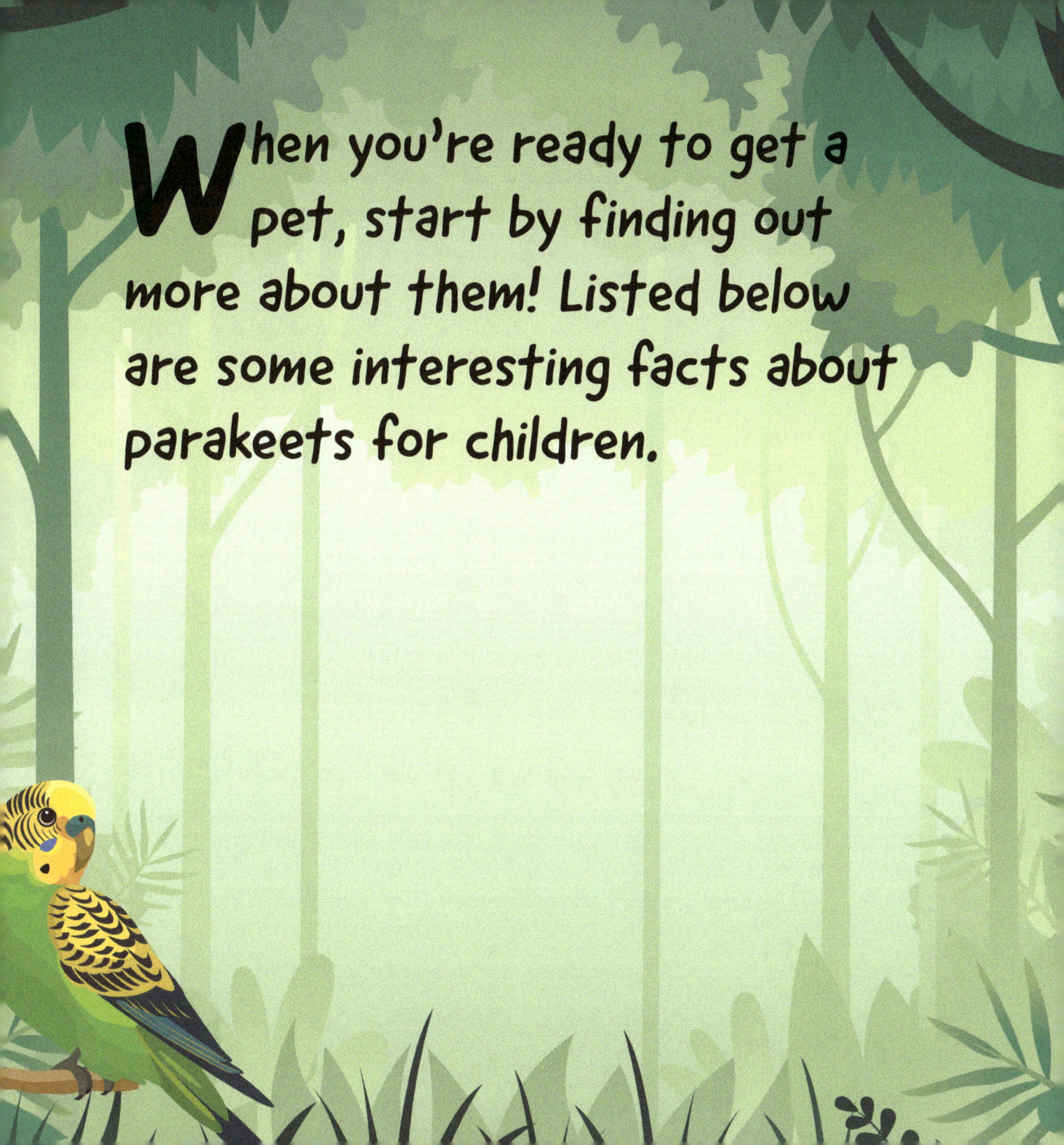

When you're ready to get a pet, start by finding out more about them! Listed below are some interesting facts about parakeets for children.

A parakeet's cere reveals its gender. The cere of a male parakeet is blue while the cere of a female parakeet is brown.

They love playing with toys and foraging for food, and you can also use them to practice counting and identifying colors. Unlike some other pets, parakeets don't use their feet to hold food.

A parakeet is a member of the parrot family, but unlike many parrots, it's smaller and less expensive. They can even learn tricks, like counting, by watching TV or using a remote control.

This little bird is native to Australia and is one of the few that live in the outback. The species has over 120 species, but the most common type is a green or blue bird with a white or pink tail.

A parakeet can live for up to fifteen years. The average lifespan is around three to five years. They are also highly active and can mimic their owners' voices. A parakeet is often an excellent pet for children and can be a great companion.

It's easy to learn about these wonderful birds. You'll be amazed at all of the fun they bring to your home. So, go ahead and read up all the facts about them!

Although parakeets are usually green in color, they can come in various colors and have many different species. In general, they have four toes and are monogamous. A parakeet's mate is its best friend.

The bird will be loyal to its owner and will bond closely with it. Its name comes from its green cere. The cere is the part above the beak. The cere is blue in males while it is brown for females.

The basic color of a parakeet is green, but there are also many species with a variety of colors. When frightened, they will fly toward a light or window. Besides, the birds are incredibly easy to train.

You can teach them to listen to cues and perform tricks. The bird's cere also helps them recognize different things, so it can understand different words and phrases.

Among the many benefits of having a pet, the smallest of parrots is its ability to talk and sing. During the breeding season, they can be very cute, but they don't have many other abilities. They are highly intelligent.

And they can even learn tricks, including counting. They are great pets for kids of all ages. You can make them a parakeet's life and teach them all about them.

The basic color of a parakeet is green. However, you can find them in all colors, including blue and green. They can live up to 15 years, and they mimic your words. They are also highly intelligent. Some of these birds even mimic what you say.

These fascinating little birds are good pets for kids of all ages. They are highly intelligent and communicate well. They are also very vocal. Unlike parrots, they can clean their feathers at any time.

While some of these facts may be surprising, they should help you make an informed decision. If you have a kid, you may want to consider purchasing a parakeet. It is the perfect pet for small children.

Ingram Content Group UK Ltd.
Milton Keynes UK
UKHW050259050423
419584UK00013B/112